Winning Shopping Center Designs

26th International
Design and Development
Awards

International Council of Shopping Centers
New York

About the International Council of Shopping Centers

This book is based on the information submitted to the International Council of Shopping Centers 26th International Design and Development Awards program. Each shopping center featured in this book was the winner of a Design Award or a Certificate of Merit, as determined by the Awards Committee.

The International Council of Shopping Centers (ICSC) is the trade association of the shopping center industry. Serving the shopping center industry since 1957, ICSC is a not-for-profit organization with over 40,000 members in 77 countries worldwide.

ICSC members include shopping center

- owners
- developers
- managers
- marketing specialists
- leasing agents
- retailers
- researchers
- attorneys
- architects
- contractors
- consultants
- investors
- lenders and brokers
- academics
- public officials

ICSC holds more than 200 meetings a year throughout the world and provides a wide array of services and products for shopping center professionals, including publications and research data.

For more information about ICSC, contact:
International Council of Shopping Centers
1221 Avenue of the Americas, 41st Floor
New York, NY 10020-1099
www.icsc.org

This publication is designed to provide accurate and authoritative information in regard to the subject matter covered. It is sold with the understanding that the publisher is not engaged in rendering legal, accounting, or other professional services. If legal advice or other expert assistance is required, the services of a competent professional person should be sought.

—From a Declaration of Principles jointly adopted by a Committee of the American Bar Association and a Committee of Publishers.

Published by
INTERNATIONAL COUNCIL OF SHOPPING CENTERS
Publications Department
1221 Avenue of the Americas
New York, NY 10020-1099

BOOK DESIGN: Harish Patel Design, New York, NY

ICSC Catalog Number: 224

International Standard Book Number: 1-58268-029-9

Printed in China

Contents

About the ICSC International Design and Development Awards

The ICSC International Design and Development Awards Program was established to recognize outstanding shopping center projects and to provide information on them to the entire industry so that others may benefit from the experiences of their colleagues.

The 26th International Design and Development Awards Program was worldwide in scope. Participation in other ICSC design awards programs, such as the Canadian or European awards, did not preclude eligible projects from being considered for an International Design and Development Award.

Projects that opened within the 18-month period, January 1, 2000, to June 30, 2001, were eligible for entry into this year's Awards Program.

Awards Categories

Categories for entries were:

Category A—Renovation or Expansion of an Existing Project
Entries had to relate to a project involving an entire shopping center, such as an enclosure, or a single facet of a center, such as an addition. The renovation or expansion must have been completed and the center fully opened for business within the 18-month period, January 1, 2000, to June 30, 2001. Eligible subject matter included, but was not limited to, improving the use of existing space, methods of keeping a center open during construction, new marketing and re-leasing approaches, refinancing techniques, innovative design and construction approaches, and adaptive reuse of the structure.

Category B—Innovative Design and Construction of a New Project
Entries had to relate to a specific new shopping center, completed and opened within the 18-month period, January 1, 2000, to June 30, 2001, and must have demonstrated how a specific design or construction problem was solved or how new standards in design or construction were established. New methods of environmental enhancement, space utilization design themes, energy conservation and innovative construction techniques were among the subjects that were considered for this category. Entries included detailed information about the

design and construction of the center, such as explanations of the reasons for, and the realized accomplishments of, the particular approach.

Awards Classifications

Entries submitted for either **category** were judged according to the following center **classification** system:

1. Projects under 150,000 square feet of total retail space*

2. Projects of 150,001 to 500,000 square feet of total retail space*

3. Projects over 500,001 square feet of total retail space.*

*Total retail space includes all square footage included in gross leasable areas (GLA), all department store or other anchor square footage, movie theaters, ice skating rinks, entertainment centers and all peripheral (out-lot) space engaged in retail enterprise. It does not include office or hotel square footage.

Eligibility

1. The ICSC International Design and Development Awards Program was open only to ICSC member companies. Any ICSC member company could enter as many projects as desired in either of the two categories.

2. Entries must have had the authorization and signature of the owner or management company of the property.

3. Projects opened within the 18-month period, January 1, 2000, to June 30, 2001, were eligible.

4. Projects must have been completed and opened for business by June 30, 2001.

5. Separate phases of a project could be submitted individually, provided they were completed and opened for business by June 30, 2001.

6. Projects could only be submitted once. Projects that were entered in the past could not be resubmitted unless substantial changes were made since the last submission.

7. Members entering the ICSC Canadian or ICSC European awards programs had to submit separately to the International Design and Development Awards Program, and entries had to adhere to its entry guidelines and requirements. Entries accepted into other ICSC awards programs did not automatically qualify for this program, nor was any entry excluded simply because it was an award winner in another program.

If you have any questions about the International Council of Shopping Centers International Design and Development Awards, or would like to receive an application for the upcoming awards program, please contact:

International Council of Shopping Centers
International Design and Development Awards
1221 Avenue of the Americas, 41st Floor
New York, NY 10020-1099
(646) 728-3462
www.icsc.org

Foreword

The worldwide recognition of outstanding projects forms the basis of the ICSC International Design and Development Awards Program. Truly reflecting the international nature of the shopping center industry, 35 percent of this year's 52 entries came from 14 countries outside of the U.S.

Most of the entries from the mature markets (U.S., Canada, Australia, Japan and western Europe) were "Renovations" of existing centers — as owners and retailers struggle to add more excitement to older shopping center formats. Reflecting today's realities of market share pressures and NOI growth needs, many of these renovations targeted limited capital investment on anchors (additions or replacements), amenities (food and play areas) and improvements to common areas. Significant additions to GLA were rare, as owners press for improved sales productivity from existing space.

The growing interest in mixed-use projects and lifestyle centers was reflected this year in U.S. and international entries. Innovative projects in Europe and Australia included drive-in theaters, I-Max theaters, bowling facilities and hotels with their retail presentations. The U.S. entries ranged from a small street retail addition to an old, established urban mall to new developments integrating street retail with more conventional mall environments. The ICSC's historic standard of excellence was reflected this year in the four Design Award winners and the 16 Certificate of Merit recipients.

The International Design and Development Awards Jury Committee is composed of 11 industry leaders from development, retailing, architecture, financial investment and consulting firms. They average in excess of 25 years' experience each and invest many hours in judging each year's submissions. I am very grateful to them for their dedication and professionalism.

This book represents the winning submissions in this year's International Design and Development Awards Program in its 26th year. We thank the entrants for their creativity, resourcefulness and hard work. We hope this recognition inspires future projects providing world-class shopping and entertainment experiences.

Daryl K. Mangan
Colonial Properties Trust

Chairman
ICSC 2002 International Design and Development Awards Jury Committee

Acknowledgments

The International Council of Shopping Centers 26th International Design and Development Awards were selected by a committee of diverse shopping center professionals representing retailers, developers and architects. The International Council of Shopping Centers is grateful to these judges for the time, effort and expertise they contributed to the awards program.

Daryl K. Mangan, *Chairman*
Colonial Properties Trust
Birmingham, Alabama

Ronald A. Altoon, FAIA
Altoon + Porter Architects
Los Angeles, California

Stanley C. Burgess
The Rouse Company
Columbia, Maryland

F. Carl Dieterle, Jr.
Simon Property Group
Indianapolis, Indiana

Gordon T. Greeby
GCI-ProNet Midwest
Lake Bluff, Illinois

John M. Millar, SCSM
Jones Lang LaSalle
Atlanta, Georgia

Matthew Ostrower
Morgan Stanley Dean Witter
New York, New York

J. Thomas Porter
Thompson, Ventulett, Stainback & Associates
Atlanta, Georgia

Rao K. Sunku
J.C. Penney Co., Inc.
Dallas, Texas

Ian F. Thomas
Thomas Consultants, Inc.
Vancouver, British Columbia

Gerald M. White
Copaken, White & Blitt
Leawood, Kansas

Owner:

F. Kemper Freeman, Jr.
Bellevue, Washington, United States

Management Company:

Bellevue Square Managers, Inc.
Bellevue, Washington, United States

Architect/Designer:

Sclater Partners Architects
(Crate and Barrel portion designed by
Crate and Barrel)
Seattle, Washington, United States

General Contractor:

Baugh Construction
Seattle, Washington, United States

The Corner at Bellevue Square

Bellevue, Washington, United States

Gross size of center:
1,300,000 sq. ft.

Amount of space added or renovated:
110,000 sq. ft.

Gross leasable area excluding anchors:
668,978 sq. ft.

Total acreage of site:
34 acres

Type of center:
Super-regional center

Physical description:
Enclosed two-level shopping center

Location of trading area:
Suburban

Population:
- Primary trading area
  1,760,000

- Secondary trading area
  1,776,000

- Annualized percentage of shoppers
  anticipated to be from outside trade area
  7%

Development schedule:
- Original opening date
  Enclosed in 1981

- Current expansion date
  Completed April 2001

Parking spaces:
- Present number
  6,000

- 476 parking spaces added in expansion

The Corner at Bellevue Square is a 110,000-square-foot, L-shaped in-fill wrapped around two sides of an existing six-story parking garage. It borders two arterial streets and leads pedestrians from one of Washington State's busiest intersections to two anchor stores of the Bellevue Square super-regional shopping center.

The new building connects to Bellevue Square via two sky bridges. It serves as a visual buffer to the concrete garage and orients its storefronts to the adjacent streets, rather than the inward look usually found at regional

The Borders Books and Music storefront uses brick, precast concrete and plaster in many colors and textures to create a bright building facade.

The Lodge's fireplace attracts pedestrians from a busy intersection to The Corner.

Destination eateries such as Starbucks Coffee and P. F. Chang's China Bistro serve customers from the street and the shopping center.

Extensive use of glass makes The Lodge part of the downtown street scene.

shopping centers. The outward focus complements the shopping center's master plan to break down barriers that sometimes isolate interior retail space from the exterior streetscape.

Public access is gained through The Lodge, a 4,000-square-foot common area that houses the high-speed elevators connecting the building to the six-level garage. The Lodge's focal point is a 40-foot-tall fireplace fashioned from Montana stone. The Lodge features rustic steel grates and a heavy steel mantle. The space is enhanced by custom-made leather furniture, distinctive lamps, coffee tables and sofa-back tables.

MAJOR TENANTS		
NAME	TYPE	GLA (SQ. FT.)
Crate and Barrel	Housewares	37,072
Borders Books and Music	Bookstore	28,000
P. F. Chang's China Bistro	Restaurant	6,290

Crate and Barrel's in-house designers created the store's exterior (below and left) to match the chain's national prototype.

The Lodge has become a popular community gathering spot.

The designers, seeking to blend The Corner's exterior with the entertainment, apartment, hotel and business edifices nearby, chose six distinct building facades, creating storefronts of brick, stone, wood, plaster and glass. These exterior facades include several destination restaurants that serve in-city residents living within walking distance.

The building rests at a busy intersection, creating opportunities for retailers new to the area. Two of them, P. F. Chang's China Bistro and Crate and Barrel, represent their chains' first locations in the state. The introduction of Crate and Barrel to the Northwest promised enough attention that Bellevue Square supported the store's opening with its own campaign. Crate and Barrel's in-house architects designed the store's exterior to match the store's national design prototype.

The fireplace in The Lodge towers 40 feet above customers.

The directories in The Lodge emulate those in recreational cabins, which show off natural artifacts. Exteriors (right) used a variety of materials, including stone, brick, glass, wood and plaster. The Lodge's custom-made lanterns (below) are over five feet tall.

The covered walkways ("The Lodge Walk") that connect The Corner to Bellevue Square use glass-covered awnings, hanging baskets and potted landscaping.

Interior signage proved an important and unanticipated aspect of making The Corner shopper-friendly. Over 75 percent of the mall's parking is across the mall from The Corner. Shoppers needed extensive signage to guide them through the mall to The Corner. The signage, which featured The Lodge's icon and motif, also announced new tenants at The Corner as they opened.

The Corner has increased pedestrian traffic and added texture and scale to the street scene, while providing a catalyst for further retail development as the area urbanizes.

Owner and Management Company:
Westcor
Phoenix, Arizona, United States

Architect/Designer:
Callison
Seattle, Washington, United States

General Contractor:
Roche Constructors, Inc.
Greeley, Colorado, United States

FlatIron Crossing
Broomfield, Colorado, United States

Gross size of center:
1,500,000 sq. ft.

Gross leasable area excluding anchors:
742,759 sq. ft.

Total acreage of site:
147 acres

Type of center:
Super-regional center

Physical description:
Two-level enclosed mall and
open-air village

Location of trading area:
Suburban

Population:
- Primary trading area
  482,842

- Secondary trading area
  833,429

- Annualized percentage of shoppers
  anticipated to be from outside trade area
  8.2%

Development schedule:
- Opening date
  August 2000

Parking spaces:
- Present number
  6,500

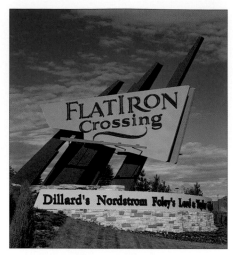

FlatIron Crossing's five anchors are spread out along the curved mall area, while the village shops comprise their own wing. Signage (right) incorporates the raw materials of the landscape and the quirky personality of the nearby Route 66.

Local authenticity and a community focus informed the design of FlatIron Crossing in the Denver suburb of Broomfield, Colorado. The 1.5 million-square-foot center combines a two-level enclosed mall, anchor tenants and a low-rise, open-air village-style collection of retail, service and food outlets.

To garner customer loyalty and attract employees, the designers sought to create an identity, look and amenities consistent with the adjacent community's lifestyle, cultural aspirations and environmental sensitivity. The center has an outdoor shopping area and two areas of park-like green space. The outdoor areas offer access to local trail systems, as well as lush landscaping, water elements and outdoor dining opportunities.

Unlike many malls, which use a rectilinear mall plan, FlatIron Crossing is laid out in two sweeping curves, which link the airy, enclosed structure with the outdoor setting. Five anchor tenants are spread about along the curved plan. The village is clearly visible from passing roadways.

FlatIron Crossing sought to complement and capitalize on its surroundings in many ways. It is oriented to take advantage of winter sunlight and diminish the effects of intense summer heat. Garage doors provide natural

Extensive use of glass brings natural daylight into FlatIron Crossing.

ventilation. Windows and clerestories are located to maximize daylight and the scenery. Native landscaping, recycled materials and locally available stone were used throughout the site.

A feature entrance is placed to capture spectacular views of the Rocky Mountains. It begins a sequence of spaces that include a sheltered meadow and pond and

MAJOR TENANTS

NAME	TYPE	GLA (SQ. FT.)
Dillards	Department store	193,440
Foley's	Department store	192,000
Nordstrom	Department store	159,360
Lord & Taylor	Department store	115,200
Galyan's	Sporting goods	97,241

Comfortable furnishings, artisan light features and recycled oak floors lend a sense of intimacy among the stores.

In the village area, tenant storefronts open onto a meandering path containing sheltered public spaces, ponds and native plantings.

ends in a four-acre park that incorporates a waterfall, native vegetation, prairie views and a nearby trail system.

Ties to the community are enhanced through the work of the FlatIron Crossing Music and Art Foundation, believed to be the first nonprofit organization established by a regional shopping center to benefit a single cause on an ongoing basis. The foundation is dedicated to preserving and protecting Colorado's music and art programs, and has distributed $50,000 in grants to date.

The center's other innovations include the ZIP shuttle on its own dedicated roadway – also believed to be a first among suburban malls. The ZIP shuttle uses European vehicles running on propane to transport shoppers between three local retail establishments.

Wrought-iron railings, wood trusses and natural-stone floorings are found through the mall and the food court.

The mall (left) was sited to take advantage of great views of the Rocky Mountains. The area's casual lifestyle is reflected (below) in the use of decks, cozy chairs and a fire pit.

Inside, designers' use of wood trusses, glass, pebble-laden terraced water features and comfortable furnishings reflect the goal of blending retail with relaxation. Many pockets of intimate space enhance the human scale. FlatIron Crossing has become "the" local gathering spot, mixing dining, strolling and shopping.

Storefronts in the village area show FlatIron Crossing's goal to be at one with the surroundings.

Owner and Management Company:
The Lutgert Companies
Naples, Florida, United States

Architect/Designer:
Humphrey Rosal Architects
Naples, Florida, United States

General Contractor:
Boran Craig Barber & Engel
Naples, Florida, United States

The Promenade at Bonita Bay

Bonita Springs, Florida, United States

Gross size of center:
106,400 sq. ft.

Gross leasable area excluding anchors:
78,400 sq. ft.

Total acreage of site:
9.3 acres

Type of center:
Fashion/specialty center

Physical description:
Open mall

Location of trading area:
Suburban

Population:
- Primary trading area
  60,000
- Secondary trading area
  250,000
- Annualized percentage of shoppers anticipated to be from outside trade area
  30%

Development schedule:
- Opening date
  May 2001

Parking spaces:
- Present number
  550

Innovative Design and Construction of a New Project

The site plan at The Promenade at Bonita Bay helps traffic flow equally past all tenant fronts.

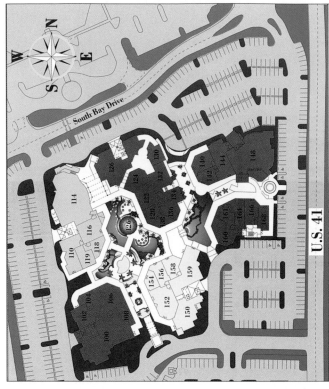

*A*n upscale mixed-use project, The Promenade at Bonita Bay includes five restaurants, 25 fashion and specialty retailers and Class-A office space. The project is the commercial centerpiece of a 3,000-acre master-planned community, voted as the nation's best by the Urban Land Institute.

An entry sign points out the center's strong suits: shopping and dining. Outdoor areas (below) take advantage of Florida's warmth and the shade of its palm trees.

Residents of two nearby affluent resort communities and the large seasonal influx of tourists both place a high priority on fine dining, so The Promenade chose to be anchored by five restaurants, which also pick up traffic from the nearly 28,000 square feet of office space. The office space was given its own key entry point at the center, with an impressive lobby, preventing the office leasers from feeling "added on" to the larger project.

The site was originally three parcels with roads bisecting each. The developer acquired the parcels and rerouted the roads, making the site suitable for a larger project. The earlier road system included easements and community-wide utilities running through what would be The

Cupolas, wrought-iron railings, tile roofs and earth tones (left) show the Italianate design concept. Water features (below) are modeled on forms found in nature.

Promenade's center courtyard. The project was designed as six separate buildings, positioned so the utility lines could be left intact.

The stores generally face inward and are interconnected by covered walkways, which meander in such a way that traffic passes by all stores so traffic flow is equalized to deter "dead spots" with lower rents. The anchor restaurants are on the outside edges of the parcels and enjoy large outdoor dining areas that add to the ambiance.

The Promenade is a destination shopping center designed in classic Mediterranean architecture, with tile roofs, pastel coloration, water features and tropical foliage. Despite the development challenges, the designers sought to make the shopper feel totally comfortable in the surroundings by avoiding "concrete canyons" and tight spaces. The Promenade's flooring patterns change constantly. Water features look natural to the environment.

Storefront signs avoid extreme graphics, instead blending with the natural elegance.

Cupolas, wrought-iron railings and earth tones reinforce the Italianate design concept. Palm trees and other natural foliage abound, providing generous shade in the Florida heat. The designers deliberately avoided extreme graphics and exaggerated storefront elements to achieve their design goal of gracious comfort for the upscale shopper and diner.

Looking back, the developer would have reversed the building process. The area facing the main highway was built last, giving the public the mistaken impression

MAJOR TENANTS		
NAME	**TYPE**	**GLA (SQ. FT.)**
South Bay Bistro	Restaurant	6,800
Houlihan's	Restaurant	6,145
Silver Spoon Café	Restaurant	5,850
Roy's	Restaurant	5,820

Building scale and paving patterns remind shoppers of residential neighborhoods rather than commercial development.

Earth and natural tones are also used in the store interiors at The Promenade at Bonita Bay.

that stores and restaurants elsewhere in the center were not yet operating. Nonetheless, upon opening, The Promenade proved that a center need not be megasized to become an exciting and stimulating retail experience.

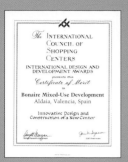

Owner and Management Company:
Riofisa and Rodamco
Madrid, Spain

Architect:
Idom Ingenieria
Madrid, Spain

Designer:
RTKL International Ltd.
Madrid, Spain

General Contractor:
Necso
Madrid, Spain

Bonaire Mixed-Use Development

Aldaia, Valencia, Spain

Gross size of center:
1,500,000 sq. ft.

Gross leasable area excluding anchors:
1,451,613 sq. ft.

Total acreage of site:
1,112 acres

Type of center:
Regional center

Physical description:
Two-level open mall

Location of trading area:
Suburban

Population:
- Primary trading area
  1,552,638

- Secondary trading area
  1,810,716

- Annualized percentage of shoppers
  anticipated to be from outside trade area
  8%

Development schedule:
- Opening date
  May 2001

Parking spaces
- Present number
  6,000

Neon and other high-concept lighting create an exciting evening look for Bonaire.

Bonaire in Aldaia, Spain, near the city of Valencia, is a mixed-use development composed of a retail and leisure district, an outlet shopping area, freestanding retail warehouses and automotive showcases, all linked by public spaces.

The site is bordered by a busy roadway and the surrounding land use is primarily industrial. The designers knew it was important to commit the center's spaces to purposes, bringing a sense of scale and orientation to the visitor. The retail/entertainment center and outlet center look inward; the warehouses are nearer the site perimeter and parking.

Bonaire's main entrance reminds visitors of the area's nautical heritage.

Lighting fixtures stand out as invigorating design elements.

The retail and leisure center allows visitors to enjoy a sequence of four open-air spaces. The first zone is centered on fashion, with classical, dignified architectural detailing. The second area contains lifestyle retailers and a distinctively comfortable ambiance. The larger third zone emphasizes leisure time, with links to the food court and the 16-screen Warner Brothers cinema. The fourth area focuses on children's fashion and retail entertainment.

A luminescent insect lends playfulness to Bonaire's sense of fun.

Brightly colored flooring and daylight make Bonaire spacious and inviting.

MAJOR TENANTS		
NAME	**TYPE**	**GLA (SQ. FT.)**
Alcampo	Hypermarket	258,065
Warner Brothers	Movie theaters	150,538
Zara	Fashion department store	55,914

Storefronts and the food court show how Bonaire capitalizes on the bright and warm climate.

The designers used the infrastructure and public amenities to weave an understandable order into the fabric of the plan. A defined hierarchy of pedestrian and vehicular circulation, drop-off plazas, landscaping and environmental graphics brings coherence to the various elements of the master plan.

Water features, frog figurines and fish icons in the floor tiles give Bonaire a sense of place and a hint of area history.

Aldaia was traditionally the weekend "getaway" community for the city of Valencia, and the designers translated that into a concept that is fun and invigorating. Neon and other lighting effects are seen through the center. A large luminescent insect hovers over a pedestrian walkway. Water features are populated by lily pads and frog figurines. Lighting fixtures are colorful and bold, rather than recessed. Flooring uses a visual patchwork of blues, yellow, purple and red. Fish icons are found in

floor tiles and in a lively entryway display. Even the center's name — Bonaire means "good air" — suggests a desire to get away from the workaday world.

The lively design concept of Bonaire has proven to be the right one to tie together different retail approaches.

Photos ©Paul Block

Certificate of Merit

Owner:
Chancery Limited
Auckland, New Zealand

Architect:
IGNITE Limited
Auckland, New Zealand

Designer:
Grant Harris + Ricky Do + Jeremy Whelan
Auckland, New Zealand

General Contractor:
Multiplex Construction Limited
Auckland, New Zealand

The Chancery

Auckland, New Zealand

Gross size of center:
53,163 sq. ft.

Gross leasable area excluding anchors:
50,052 sq. ft.

Total acreage of site:
1,042 acres

Type of center:
Fashion/specialty center

Physical description:
Open mall

Location of trading area:
Urban Central Business District

Population:
- Primary trading area
  381,300

- Secondary trading area
  1,209,000

- Annualized percentage of shoppers anticipated to be from outside trade area
  35%

Development schedule:
- Opening date
  December 2000

Parking spaces
- Present number
  228

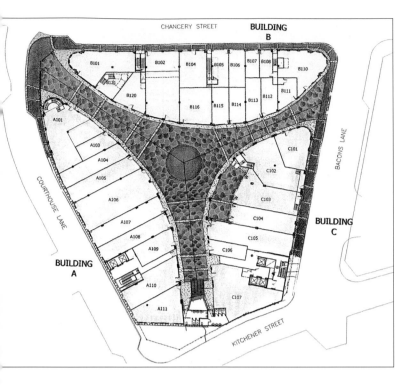

The Chancery is composed of three buildings with a common walkway between them. Poles atop domes and pyramids (below) define The Chancery's boundaries for the shopping public.

*T*he Chancery in Auckland, New Zealand, is a mixed-use development with retail and other types of commercial spaces and a parking garage. The shape of the site inspired the design of three buildings, leaving open space with sunlight between the buildings.

Curved facades create a structural environment uncommon in the area. The pedestrians-only walkway between the buildings gives maximum exposure to storefronts and creates an internal piazza, with a large glass canopy. The complex itself is defined for passersby by poles atop rooftops in dome and pyramid shapes.

MAJOR TENANTS		
NAME	**TYPE**	**GLA (SQ. FT.)**
Esprit	Fashion	3,148
Servilles	Hairdressing	1,991
Living & Giving	Gifts	1,764
Cube	Fashion	1,671
Versace Classic V2	Fashion	1,645
Satori	Fashion	1,515
Mecca	Cafe	1,108

Plantings, low-rise
buildings and clean,
crisp design create a
human scale at The
Chancery.

Signage and design components lend the new project a sense of urban history.

A major design goal was how to retain the human scale of the older buildings in the area. The developers and designers studied edifices on nearby streets, which are largely older, low-rise, small-scale office buildings. They decided that there needed to be variation within their own buildings' architectural style and that each shop facade must make an individual statement. Further, they chose to make a strong visual connection with adjacent

Freyberg Square, using canopies, seating, cafes, vegetation and shelter.

To achieve a distinct look for each retail tenant, the designers used over 40 different facade treatments, 50 types of stone finishes, 150 different types of windows and 47 separate floor levels. These gave The Chancery a variety of colors and textures within a common design concept. Throughout, there is a crisp, clean

From the central piazza, shoppers can look up to the office levels.

There is easy access to The Chancery's stores and eateries from many points in downtown Auckland.

A cafe in The Chancery's central piazza.

look. Upper-floor windows are unadorned by shutters. Colors are those found in most older urban districts: whites, brick reds, beiges and greys. Storefront displays generally allow clear views into the stores themselves, encouraging visits.

Awnings and street furniture reinforce the human scale at ground level. The stone walkway between the buildings uses a scallop-shaped pattern that sets the district apart from neighbor streets. The walkway is generously landscaped, offering shade at midday at the outdoor dining tables. The walkway itself is largely kept clear of signage, which facilitates pedestrian flow and allows design to shine. Wherever possible, design has provided open space and long views — opening the center of a multistory stairwell, for example, or accenting a sense of place with views of taller downtown buildings.

While there is an emphasis on fashion stores, there are also gift stores and services available. Traffic to the center has benefited from high-profile anchor tenants such as Versace Classic V2 and Servilles. Tenants have the opportunity to own their shop. With the mix of retail and eateries, plus the presence of office workers, university students and tourists, The Chancery makes a significant contribution to life in downtown Auckland.

Simple and unadorned, the clean look of The Chancery's architecture is built on dozens of textures, levels and colors.

Owner and Management Company:
Mitsui Fudosan
Tokyo, Japan

Architect:
Mitsui Kensetsu
Tokyo, Japan

Designer:
RTKL International Ltd.
Tokyo, Japan
Dallas, Texas, United States

General Contractor:
Mitsui Kensetsu
Tokyo, Japan

Garden Walk Makuhari

Mihama-Ku, Chiba, Japan

Gross size of center:
156,400 sq. ft.

Gross leasable area excluding anchors:
122,500 sq. ft.

Total acreage of site:
2.85 acres

Type of center:
Regional fashion/specialty outlet center

Physical description:
Two-level open mall

Location of trading area:
Suburban

Population:
• Primary trading area
 1,430,000

• Secondary trading area
 2,100,000

• Annualized percentage of shoppers
 anticipated to be from outside trade area
 50%

Development schedule:
• Opening date
 October 24, 2000

Parking spaces:
• Present number
 1,250

Innovative Design and Construction of a New Project

*G*arden Walk Makuhari is a two-story outdoor center with 59 tenants, surrounding a series of three courtyards. In Japan, many suburban sites remain undeveloped. The developer of Garden Walk has created a family of outlet malls in locations throughout Japan to use these sites temporarily. The land on which Garden Walk is built is leased for a 10- to 15-year period. The buildings are constructed of light steel framing, cross-braced against Japan's seismic dangers and sheathed with a variety of low-cost claddings such as autoclaved lightweight concrete.

The Nike logo (above) attracts shoppers at one entrance to Garden Walk, while immense art overhead (above right) draws attention at another. The center's graphics celebrate flowers as symbols of love and worship.

Art is everywhere at Garden Walk — outside and inside.

The center's design is based on flowers as symbols of worship and love and for their importance in music, poetry and art throughout history. The resulting graphic and sculptural elements are highly abstract, chic and contemporary, set against architectural expression that is simple, colorful and as modern as the flower graphics. Since Japanese contractors are willing to study and refine during actual construction, the design team was able to experiment with colors, exterior skins, plastics, signage and lighting during the building process.

A variety of shapes, sizes and colors are used in storefronts. Overhead walkways (far right) allow easy access between second-floor retailers.

MAJOR TENANTS		
NAME	**TYPE**	**GLA (SQ. FT.)**
Next Door	Apparel	7,573
Nike Factory Store	Sportswear	7,445
Adidas Factory Outlet	Sportswear	5,662
Franc Franc Bazaar	Home furnishing	5,509
mont-bell	Outdoor/sports apparel	5,497

The center is dotted with interactive fountains, glowing flowers and a giant sunflower performance enclosure. There are 15-foot-tall flower portraits and a tulip fountain with foot-long petal canopies. The three courts are tied to colors: red for the Rose Court, violet for the Tulip Court and orange for the Sunflower Court.

At left, graphic torchieres illuminate an interior court.

Photo-real posters of flowers break up the exterior façade, carrying the graphic theme to passersby.

Signature tulip sculptures announce the entryway to the family-focused Garden Walk.

Garden Walk is designed as a family experience. At the far end of the Rose Court, for example, a bouquet of 12-foot-tall roses are made of fiber-reinforced polymer, with six-foot-tall thorns. Each thorn offers a throne-like seat with private music, including such thematically appropriate songs as "La Vie en Rose" and "The Yellow Rose of Texas." On any day, children climb from thorn to thorn as they listen to all the songs.

Garden Walk attracts more than half its visitors from outside its trade area. Indeed, the design team churned through dozens of name options looking for those that resonated in both Japanese and English.

The center also provides a central point for the Makuhari area. Just 30 minutes from Tokyo, the area had been developed with offices, hotels and a convention center, but failed to offer a lifestyle-focused retail center. Garden Walk also serves as a major gateway between a rail station and a major residential neighborhood.

The developer states that, too often, Japanese retail is designed for efficiency, resulting in 10-story department stores, mom-and-pop shops or subterranean shopping plazas at train stations. Garden Walk offers a successful alternative to that, while satisfying the Japanese consumer's desire for brand-name products.

Certificate of Merit

Owner:

Lewis Land Group of Companies / ING Real Estate
Sydney, New South Wales, Australia

Management Company:

Kingridge Finance Pty., Ltd.
Sydney, New South Wales, Australia

Architect/Designer:

The Buchan Group
Brisbane, Queensland, Australia

General Contractor:

Multiplex
Brisbane, Queensland, Australia

Harbour Town Shopping Centre
Gold Coast, Queensland, Australia

Gross size of center:
500,000 sq. ft.

Gross leasable area excluding anchors:
320,000 sq. ft.

Total acreage of site:
50 acres

Type of center:
Regional center

Physical description:
Open mall

Location of trading area:
Tourist area

Population:
- Primary trading area
  234,061

- Secondary trading area
  183,905

- Annualized percentage of shoppers
  anticipated to be from outside trade area
  70%

Development schedule:
- Opening date
  December 1999

- Future expansion
  2003

Parking spaces:
- Present number
  3,000

Below, the boldness and energy of the entire center is reflected in signage at storefronts, along a roadside, at exterior facades and at a parking area.

Natural vegetation, strong graphics and interesting pavement design welcome visitors to Harbour Town.

*H*arbour Town is the first regional shopping center in Australia to provide a manufacturer's outlet shopping precinct built for that purpose. It is a single-level, open-air themed center with three distinct areas: a manufacturer's outlet, convenience shopping and entertainment/dining.

Planning presented two key challenges. First, the Gold Coast — Australia's largest regional tourism destination — already had the highest concentration of retail space per capita on the continent. Second, the site was located outside the main tourism strip. For a success, the developer and designer would have to make Harbour Town a destination of its own.

An entry to Harbour Town Shopping Center in Australia's Gold Coast shows designers succeeded in avoiding the "black-box" look of some manufacturer's outlet centers.

The designers provided an industrial look in abundance. Bold storefronts (above) and metallic sculpture (below) reinforce the design message.

The concept became a "back-to-the-streets" approach that captured the relaxed and open spirit of the Gold Coast, with open-air malls, veranda awnings and sidewalk cafes.

For the first time, the developer says, shoppers have a retail center that atmospherically evokes an era when the family "went to town" to shop. Within a contemporary framework, the streets of Harbour Town create vistas of eclectic, stylized buildings. The cinemas conjure

Thoughtful planning provides shade from the bright Gold Coast sun.

Harbour Town added cinemas and convenience shopping to the area's retail mix.

MAJOR TENANTS

NAME	TYPE	GLA (SQ. FT.)
Reading Cinemas	Movie theaters	60,000
Woolworths	Supermarket	38,880
Dimmeys	Discount department store	25,250
David Jones Warehouse	Department store	22,570
Crazy Clarks	Discount department store	12,380

Tourism accounts for 70 percent of Harbour Town's visitors, many of whom find familiar shops and logos.

The graphic effects at Harbour Town rise well above street level.

images of the heyday of the silver screen. The superpharmacy is fashioned in the art nouveau style of a traditional apothecary. The supermarket looks like an early one from the 1940s.

The "big-box" approach of some outlet malls was studiously avoided. Seven separate buildings have a range of facades and forms, connected by a common design language of bold and dynamic street architecture. Buildings are constructed primarily of simple steel-framed, flat-roofed structures of cost-effective materials, with great effect achieved through the use of shape, color and texture. Overhead links, colorful graphics and signage, pavements and landscape elements abound.

The designers were successful in their goals of providing easy access for maintenance and repair equipment at all hours and brightly lit streets and parking areas. The open-air design avoids the high cost and energy inefficiency of traditionally air-conditioned spaces. Natural ventilation and light, verandas and cross-street links provide sheltered pedestrian access in all weather and act as sun protection, reducing heat loads.

There is a "main street" with several intersecting cross-malls that lead to surrounding parking areas. Service areas are grouped in internal courtyards, screened from adjacent parking areas, but providing easy access to the rear of shops. External pavements, a mix of exposed aggregate pavers and asphaltic concrete, are robust, cost-effective and provide an appropriate look for the center.

Harbour Town also added many new types of retailers to the area — cinemas, restaurants, banking and postal facilities, medical and fitness centers and health and beauty salons. In all, Harbour Town shows how a region already dense in retail can indeed handle more retail opportunities.

Covered eating areas, whimsical transportation and artistic water features provide a memorable shopping experience at Australia's Harbour Town.

Owner and Management Company:
Inmobiliaria Mall Viña Del Mar S.A.
Viña del Mar, V Region, Chile

Architect/Designer:
Pfeifer & Zurdo Arquitectos
Buenos Aires, Capital Federal, Argentina

General Contractor:
Desco - Tecsa
Santiago, Quinta Region, Chile

Mall Marina Arauco

Viña del Mar, Quinto Region, Chile

Gross size of center:
537,000 sq. ft.

Gross leasable area excluding anchors:
100,000 sq. ft.

Total acreage of site:
5 acres

Type of center:
Regional center

Physical description:
Four-level mall

Location of trading area:
Urban but not downtown

Population:
- Primary trading area
  800,000

- Secondary trading area
  400,000

- Annualized percentage of shoppers
  anticipated to be from outside trade area
  25%

Development schedule:
- Opening date
  January 2000

- Future expansion
  December 2003

Parking spaces:
- Present number
  1,300

- 700 parking spaces added in renovation

*M*all Marina Arauco, about an hour away from Valparaiso, Chile, was built over, under and around a public street.

The surrounding area is composed of recent development that has replaced a dilapidated industrial district with high-quality residential buildings and a convenience center that includes a hypermarket and home center. Major roads adjoin the mall's site, providing excellent access to the complex. The street bisecting the two city blocks on which the center was built proved to be the major obstacle to development.

This aerial photograph shows how the two sections of Mall Marina Arauco surround the bisecting street from all perspectives.

The office floors tower above the mall and provide plenty of shoppers.

The mall ends are located at major intersections.

Nonetheless, the designers were committed to presenting an overall unity of style between the two sections of the mall. Structurally, they did so by building retail space below and above the street. The retail stores on the "ground" floor flow continuously over the two blocks and under the bisecting street. The mezzanine level is split by the street, and the three levels above contain stores, including a food court, overlooking the street.

The design adopted for the mall is a free-flowing "S" shape that crosses the floor plan diagonally, linking the two main street corners. A court at each end of the mall allows a return route to the mall, vertical circulation via escalators and elevators, and also creates a link to outdoor areas and basement parking.

MAJOR TENANTS

NAME	TYPE	GLA (SQ. FT.)
Almacenes Par's	Department store	140,000
Ripley	Department store	140,000
Cinemark Entertainment Center	Multiscreen theater	48,000

Appealing merchandise and native flora surround visitors to Mall Marina Arauco.

Approaching an entryway, shoppers are introduced to the concept of openness that guided the designers.

Innovative Design and Construction of a New Project

The mall's skylight received particular attention, since the mall is in a beach and tourist resort where the sun, sea and sky are the natural leitmotif. The designers created a glass cover borne by a metal structure made of cross beams of different lengths that mimics the wide curves of the pedestrian circulation pattern. The color of the glass, say the designers, closely matches the color of the nearby Pacific waters. The center's visual openness was further enhanced by use of transparent indoor-outdoor partitions at the courts.

Multistory views and the grand S-shape of the major mall walkway reflect the relaxed nature of the beachfront community.

The food court occupies the center section of the second floor.

The lively design of Mall Marina Arauco created a successful community gathering place.

A pedestrian bridge was built between Mall Marina Arauco and the adjacent convenience center, which contains a hypermarket and a home center. The bridge creates a three-block shopping district for residents, tourists and the workers in the office building that makes up part of the Mall Marina Arauco.

Owner and Management Company:
Wessman Development Company
Palm Springs, California, United States

Architect/Designer:
Altevers Associates
San Diego, California, United States

General Contractor:
R.D. Olson Construction
Irvine, California, United States

Mercado Plaza

Palm Springs, California, United States

Gross size of center:
37,603 sq. ft.

Gross leasable area excluding anchors:
35,925 sq. ft.

Total acreage of site:
.57 acres

Type of center:
Fashion/specialty neighborhood center

Physical description:
Two-level

Location of trading area:
Urban

Population:
- Primary trading area
  42,000

- Secondary trading area
  300,000

- Annualized percentage of shoppers
  anticipated to be from outside trade area
  25–30%

Development schedule:
- Opening date
  January 2000

Parking spaces:
- Present number
  150

Mercado Plaza's design was part of a revitalization effort to bring the Mediterranean-style "Old Palm Springs" look back to downtown. The two buildings (above) are easily accessible to pedestrians.

The Palm Springs, California, site on which Mercado Plaza rose previously held an abandoned building — a gap in the pedestrian experience of this legendary community. Downtown development since the 1930s had been more modern than the "Old Palm Springs" look (a Mediterranean style), and the city had launched a revitalization effort to restore the old style.

The developer envisioned a marketplace that would complement and enhance the revitalization work and set a new standard in the community in quality of materials and aesthetic appeal. The re-creation of historic Palm Springs would be part of the challenge in the development of this half-acre plot as a specialty retail/office complex of two, two-story Mediterranean-style buildings separated by a courtyard.

Mercado Plaza's entrance and walkways were designed to provide direct access both from the town's main shopping strip and from a 150-space parking lot behind the plaza. A footbridge at the rear of the plaza's courtyard connects the center's two buildings and offers a direct view of Palm Springs' desert mountains.

Mercado Plaza's "village" design incorporates Mediterranean architectural elements such as stone columns, trellis-covered terraces, balconies and awnings. Its most noticeable features are the details and materials on the exterior of the buildings. French doors lead to terraces. Twelve different shades of lime wash were painted on the exterior of the plaza. Railings are handcrafted

MAJOR TENANTS		
NAME	**TYPE**	**GLA (SQ. FT.)**
The Falls Martini Bar & Steakhouse	Restaurant	5,892
Ruby's Restaurant	Restaurant	4,115

Storeowners were encouraged to use signage styles different from their neighbors. Art galleries and boutiques are among the upscale tenants. Wrought-iron and Cantera stone (right) highlight the design.

Awnings of contrasting colors and palm trees (right) each make their own design statement.

from wrought iron, as is the decorative hardware that secures awnings and light fixtures. Balconies of varying shapes and sizes are covered by awnings of contrasting colors.

Custom-made light fixtures, fabricated of copper and glass and fashioned in an old-world style, line the perimeter of the courtyard and the front of the plaza. Cantera stone complements many building elements, including the second-level columns and framing on the windows and storefronts. To add to the ambiance, the developer and architect encouraged tenants to use pedestrian-scale signage that differed from neighboring stores.

The tenant mix is upscale and includes art galleries, restaurants, specialty-apparel boutiques, gift shops and a congresswoman's office. The developer says that, had he the chance to re-do the project, he would expand it by including adjacent properties, an initiative that began after the center opened.

The Santa Rosa Mountains provide a dramatic backdrop for Mercado Plaza.

Due to its central location – close to many tourist attractions – and its success at bringing back the "Old Palm Springs" style, Mercado Plaza serves as a "something for everyone" destination for shopping and dining.

Certificate of Merit

Owner and Management Company:

Sadyba Center S.A.
Warsaw, Poland

Architect/Designer:

Pawel W. Gralinski
Warsaw, Poland

General Contractor:

Hochtief Poland S.A.
Warsaw, Poland

Sadyba Best Mall

Warsaw, Poland

Gross size of center:
279,864 sq. ft.

Gross leasable area excluding anchors:
166,552 sq. ft.

Total acreage of site:
6.87 acres

Type of center:
Neighborhood/regional center

Physical description:
Enclosed mall

Location of trading area:
Urban

Population:
• Primary trading area
  150,000

• Secondary trading area
  2,000,000

• Annualized percentage of shoppers
  anticipated to be from outside trade area
  10%

Development schedule:
• Opening date
  September 2000

• Future expansion
  Autumn 2004

Parking spaces:
• Present number
  1,015

• 550 parking spaces to be added in
  extension

Neon and an undulating exterior exemplify the modern design of Sadyba Best Mall in Warsaw.

*T*he primary market for Sadyba Best Mall in Warsaw held great potential for a regional mall. The mall is located on a main thoroughfare and surrounded by residential complexes in the Mokotóv district, the biggest and most densely populated area of Warsaw. The mall's primary market has the highest average per capita income and the highest level of education.

The lack of commercial development in the area encouraged the developers to create a three-level center with broad public appeal: fashion, supermarket, recreation and cinemas all under one roof. The location was sufficiently appealing to attract the first IMAX theater in central Europe, a welcome addition to the planned 12-screen cinema.

The IMAX structure is attached to the main mall by a bridge. The high-tech design cleverly masks air vents in the cones near the roof.

Illumination is enhanced by an artificial skylight that stretches the length of the mall.

Design of store interiors complements that of the mall area.

Entertainment retailers, including the cinemas and a 20-lane bowling alley, are located on the third level of the building, to draw traffic flow upwards and guarantee that visitors would have to travel through the mall area and the first-floor food court after the movie. The IMAX itself is in a separate building connected to the main edifice by a bridge. The IMAX has no direct outside entrance, requiring its customers to enter the center proper.

The mall area of the lower two retail floors shows a unified interior design and is lit by an artificial skylight for its entire length. The ground floor is anchored by a supermarket and a leading retailer. The first floor holds small fashion anchors and the food court.

The exterior presents a variety of shapes and colors to passersby — a significant difference from the metallic squared edifices of retail developments in the area. In designing the facade, care was taken to create small-scale detail that would not detract from the surrounding neighborhood. Most parking is hidden beneath the building on one level, stretching

Bridges over the central mall maximize access to second-floor retailers.

MAJOR TENANTS

NAME	TYPE	GLA (SQ. FT.)
Cinema City	Multiplex theater	56,995
Hokus & Pokus	Entertainment center	32,055
Champion	Supermarket	30,774

the whole of the property, although 350 spaces are located in front of the building to communicate parking availability to tourists and newcomers. There is no "back side" in the mall's design.

The interior design features highly polished stone and tile surfaces in hues of eggshell and brown. Storefront signage is tightly controlled, to maximize visual appeal of the mall overall.

The cinema lobby (above and right) offers dramatic design.

Since the opening of Sadyba, two more malls have opened in Poland and 40 new projects are scheduled in the next five years.
Nonetheless, an extension is already planned for Sadyba, which has been widely acclaimed for its pleasant atmosphere and its appeal as a community gathering place.

The food court and 20-lane bowling alley add to the appeal of Sadyba Best Mall.

Owner:
Riofisa
Salamanca, Spain

Management Company:
Riofisa
Madrid, Spain

Architect:
Antonio Fernandez Alba
Madrid, Spain

Designer:
RTKL International Ltd.
Madrid, Spain

General Contractor:
Eralan S.A.
Madrid, Spain

Salamanca Train Station

Salamanca, Salamanca, Spain

Gross size of center:
322,580 sq. ft.

Gross leasable area excluding anchors:
120,000 sq. ft.

Total acreage of site:
7.4 acres

Type of center:
Community center

Physical description:
Enclosed two-level mall

Location of trading area:
Urban

Population:
- Primary trading area
  196,265
- Secondary trading area
  27,038
- Annualized percentage of shoppers anticipated to be from outside trade area
  2.8%

Development schedule:
- Opening date
  March 2001

Parking spaces:
- Present number
  800

Innovative Design and Construction of a New Project

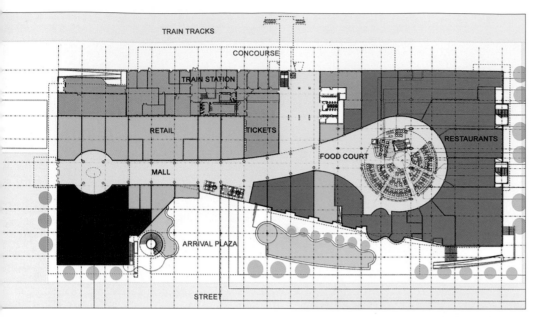

The transit station lies at upper left in this site plan for Salamanca Train Station shopping mall.

The "blanket" roof of the exterior plaza (above and right) blazes color at night, hinting at the recreational and entertainment activity found inside.

*S*alamanca Train Station is a retail development that wraps around an existing train station. Its inventive approach to mixed use, combining leisure and transportation, provides the surrounding city with a new public space.

A number of design challenges were successfully met. By the time the designer was brought in, the building was under construction and over budget. The design needed to absorb the work that had already been done.

Further, the rail authority required a formal and institutional expression for the building's exterior. The developer sought a more playful look, consistent with the proposed leisure focus of the center, perhaps using a variety of shapes, colors and forms.

The design team incorporated both concepts. The building, clad in Salamanca stone, projects a formal air by day, signifying one's arrival at the train station. By night, however, colorful lighting creates a special effect, changing the center into a livelier environment.

The façade of the retail center creates a new address and signage for the train station.

Crucial to this duality is the center's exterior plaza, an outdoor foyer that offers a large public space for celebrations, gatherings and other uses. The developer says that the plaza serves as a hinge between the day and night design concepts. The plaza is covered by a "blanket" ceiling that uses strategic lighting at night to change its color from red to yellow to blue. The building also includes a tower that appears to look like a simple cone during the day, but changes color at night to create a visual landmark for the city of Salamanca.

Graphics (above and right) are kept small and discreet, so as not to distract from the neighborhood.

Abundant natural light washes over the mall area. At far right, the cone rises from the exterior plaza — majestic by day, colorful at night.

The key to Salamanca's successful design was in matching the scale of the city and the neighborhood. The retail building enhances and complements the town, rather than overwhelming it. The designers adapted this concept inside the mall as well: transit-oriented retail shops, are sized smaller than those in traditional malls.

Leasing decisions at Salamanca focused on the types of merchandise that might be of interest to both travelers and local residents. Store location was decided largely by the type of shopper each would attract: retailers targeting train riders are placed closest to the transit access, and leisure-type shopping is located farther away.

The plaza (left) serves as access for shoppers and train riders. A variety of skylight treatments (above) adds diversity to the design look.

MAJOR TENANTS

NAME	TYPE	GLA (SQ. FT.)
Premiere Megaplex	Cinemas	31,183
Champion	Supermarket	19,355
Burger King	Fast food restaurant	4,301

The plaza has become an important community gathering place for young and old.

Retail at Salamanca Train Station is kept to the smaller scale typically found at transit facilities.

The developer credits the center's success to the collaboration between public and private sectors, building on cross-fertilization of the government's assessment of civic needs with the developer's evaluation of shopping and leisure needs.

In addition to the exterior plaza, a food court and music court also serve as community gathering places, helping Salamanca Train Station transform its neighborhood with new public space for the city, a new address for the train station and new retailers.

Photos ©Paul Block

The INTERNATIONAL COUNCIL OF SHOPPING CENTERS
INTERNATIONAL DESIGN AND DEVELOPMENT AWARDS
presents this
Certificate of Merit
to
The Shops at North Bridge
Chicago, Illinois, United States
Innovative Design and
Construction of a New Center

The Shops at North Bridge

Chicago, Illinois, United States

Owner:
RN 124/125 Company, LLC
c/o The John Buck Company
Chicago, Illinois, United States

Management Company:
The John Buck Company
Chicago, Illinois, United States

Architect/Designer:
Anthony Belluschi Architects
(Now known as OWP/P Belluschi Architects)
Chicago, Illinois, United States

General Contractor:
AMEC Construction
Management Inc.
Chicago, Illinois, United States

Gross size of center:
212,000 sq. ft.

Gross leasable area excluding anchors:
114,284 sq. ft.

Total acreage of site:
1.07 acres

Type of center:
Fashion/specialty center

Physical description:
Five-level urban mall

Location of trading area:
Urban Central Business District

Population:
- Primary trading area
  N/A

- Secondary trading area
  N/A

- Annualized percentage of shoppers
  anticipated to be from outside trade area
  50%

Development schedule:
- Opening date
  December 2000

Parking spaces:
- Present number N/A

The Shops at North Bridge created frontage on the "Magnificent Mile" for the first Nordstrom in downtown Chicago.

*T*he Shops at North Bridge links Chicago's famous "Magnificent Mile" shopping avenue to a new upscale hotel and the first Nordstrom department store in downtown Chicago.

The shops are reached through a retail arcade: a five-story steel and glass atrium accented with a hanging dichroic light-refracting glass sculpture. At one end of the arcade is the "Magnificent Mile" section of Michigan Avenue. At the other is Nordstrom, located a block off the avenue. The curved retail arcade, designed with contrasting solids and voids on opposite sides, evokes a winding European street. Specialty and fashion shops are arranged along the gently rising path.

A light-refracting glass sculpture (left) hangs in the five-story atrium. Pedestrian bridges (right) connect walkways throughout the mall.

To bring this about, the developer and design team completed what is believed to be the tallest dismantlement and reconstruction of a landmark facade in North America: reconstructing the 1929 art-deco McGraw-Hill building. The original design for The Shops at North Bridge had to be modified after the McGraw-Hill facade received landmark status in 1998. The older building's original grid would not accommodate hotel or retail space, so the facade's limestone was carefully removed, the old structure torn down, a new steel structure placed and the original limestone rehung on the new structure.

Over 4,850 Indiana limestone pieces, ranging from two-foot strips to seven-foot square blocks weighing as much as 9,000 pounds, were individually

Four of the zodiac-themed limestone panels (above) form a display within the center. A food court (left) comprises an entire floor.

The scale within the center permits the use of dramatic sculpture.

MAJOR TENANT

NAME	TYPE	GLA (SQ. FT.)
Nordstrom *(adjacent to project)*	Department store	260,000

Interiors were designed to allow clear, wide views within the mall area.

Furnishings reflect the art-deco theme of the original facade.

catalogued, repaired, cleaned and reinstalled, largely in their original locations, on the new steel structure. The team was able to reuse 98 percent of the original limestone in the reconstructed portion.

The original facade showed zodiac-themed panels by 20th-century sculptor Gwen Lux. Four of the handcarved limestone panels, which could not be returned to their original locations, now form a historical display just off the main atrium. The display serves as a focal point for the interior and links it to the exterior. Granite flooring and Italian limestone add richness to the space and unify the design.

The Shops at North Bridge is part of a large redevelopment project designed to "bridge" the North Michigan Avenue district with the River North/Rush Street entertainment area. The contemporary design of the atrium and arcade is both a contrast and a complement to the historic building, using a similar color palette and materials.

The project maximized the tight site by building the luxury hotel over the retail space and using air rights over Grand Avenue and Rush Street. Limitations on these air rights required vehicular and truck clearance on the two streets, as well as a large public glass-covered atrium. Merchandising was restricted within the air-rights parcels.

Finally, 28 trees and 35 plantings were added to the two urban blocks, which previously had no greenery. Wider sidewalks, taxi drop-off locations, sidewalk medallions, ornamental iron elements and engraved building plaques all add to the appeal of The Shops at North Bridge.

Highly finished surfaces add an elegant touch to the design of The Shops at North Bridge.

Certificate of Merit

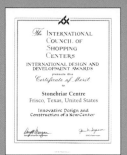

Owner:

Stonebriar Mall Partnership/ General Growth Properties, Inc.

Management Company:

General Growth Properties, Inc.
Chicago, Illinois, United States

Architect/Designer:

ELS Architecture and Urban Design
Berkeley, California, United States

General Contracor:

Vratsinas Construction Company
Little Rock, Arkansas, United States

Stonebriar Centre

Frisco, Texas, United States

Gross size of center:
1,566,144 sq. ft.

Gross leasable area excluding anchors:
528,000 sq. ft.

Total acreage of site:
106.45 acres

Type of center:
Super-regional center

Physical description:
Two-level enclosed mall with third-level cinema

Location of trading area:
Suburban

Population:
- Primary trading area
  331,500

- Secondary trading area
  N/A

- Annualized percentage of shoppers anticipated to be from outside trade area
  20%

Development schedule:
- Opening date
  August 4, 2000

Parking spaces:
- Present number
  7,215

Exterior signage provides visibility for restaurants at Stonebriar Centre near Dallas.

The varied and curved rooflines (right) and the use of neon and color (below) hint at the fun-focused family environment located within.

Stonebriar Centre is a super-regional three-level mall designed as a place for families to shop and be entertained. The project includes five anchor department stores, one sports anchor, a 24-screen cinema, an ice rink, a 950-seat food court and 160 specialty stores and restaurants. Two cities in the rapidly developing market north of Dallas, Texas, competed for the center, which was finally opened in Frisco.

Texas-style icons (left) dominate the food court, while a crisp, clean look (opposite) dominates the main interior.

Natural light is abundant in the center, and glazed glass cuts down on the hot Dallas sun.

The development process paid special attention to vehicular access and parking. All site work was designed with the understanding that an elevated interchange is planned in conjunction with improvements by the Texas Highway Department. New and improved access roads and continuous way-finding signage were provided. Parking lots included two-foot candle lighting. Hot summer days and the developer's request for valet services prompted the architects and designers to provide a 680-car covered parking area that feeds customers into the lower mall area. Other parking leads to the upper-level shops and center court. Use of two-level parking provides good vehicular circulation. A water-retention pond and accommodation for fast runoff flow helps clear rainfall from the 110-acre parking area.

Leasing demands resulted in signage for "big-box" retailers (such as restaurants, bookstores and others) being posted onto the outside of the center. The developer reports this was a very successful move, since the well-known restaurant signage and the

MAJOR TENANTS

NAME	TYPE	GLA (SQ. FT.)
Macy's	Department store	210,000
Foley's	Department store	200,000
JC Penney	Department store	165,000
Sears	Department store	149,965
Nordstrom	Department store	143,200
AMC Cinemas	Multiplex cinema	96,560
Galyan's	Sporting goods store	77,411
Ice arena	Recreation	34,412

The play area and soft seating complement the center's family focus.

A two-story professional-size ice rink, free Internet hook-ups at the Byte Site and a large carousel give families lots to do beyond shopping.

facade of the two-story ice arena present a powerful street image that will not be overpowered by the flyover interchange when it is built in a few years.

The focus on family resulted in several beneficial developments. The large food court includes a pavilion with walk-up Internet-access stations. Food court murals feature historical images of the Frisco area, and photographic memorabilia are enclosed in tabletops. The two-story main mall entrances are flanked by exterior-accessed restaurants. Family-equipped rest rooms are on two levels. An electronic screen lists "Frisco Activity" nearby. A large custom-made carousel and carpeted soft-seating areas also attract families. A local sponsor subsidized a children's soft-sided play area.

A professional-size ice rink area includes party rooms and dressing rooms to incorporate all types of skating activity: family skating, lessons, free skate and organized hockey team play. Upper-level "skybox" seating and food court tables overlook the rink below.

Placement of the multiscreen cinema alone on the third floor means that a long queue for tickets does not obstruct traffic in the main mall area. The developer sees now, however, that the cinema level could handle double its two current restaurants and that a larger elevator would be more accommodating to people requiring access for wheelchairs and baby carriages, who are heavy users of the facilities. The public restrooms near the children's soft play space also need to be enlarged. These concerns, however, are a happy result of the wide acceptance of Stonebriar Center by area families.

Frosted-glass railing walls, a Texas-themed mural and decorated food court tabletops entertain the eye at Stonebriar Centre.

Photos: Timothy Hursley
Architectural graphic design: Redmond Schwartz Design Inc.

Owner:
Yoku Moku Co., Ltd.
Tokyo, Japan

Management Company:
Takenaka Corporation
Tokyo, Japan

Architect/Designer:
Takenaka Corporation
Tokyo, Japan

General Contractor:
Takenaka Corporation
Tokyo, Japan

YM Square Harajuku

Tokyo, Japan

Gross size of center:
64,547 sq. ft.

Gross leasable area excluding anchors:
40,031 sq. ft.

Total acreage of site:
0.5 acres

Type of center:
Fashion/specialty center

Physical description:
Six-level freestanding center

Location of trading area:
Urban

Population:
• Primary trading area
  1.8 million

• Secondary trading area
  10 million

• Annualized percentage of shoppers
  anticipated to be from outside trade area
  20%

Development schedule:
• Opening date
  January 27, 2001

Parking spaces:
• Present number
  28

*T*he design concept for YM Square Harajuku in downtown Tokyo is an "urban showcase." The six-floor project's flagship stores are on display to pedestrians through a glass skin facade with distinctive vertical mullions. The center mixes fashion/specialty retailers and eateries.

The half-acre size of the plot and Japanese law determined much of the decision-making about design. There is a passageway through the center of the building to maximize circulation between a trendy side street and the main

The exterior of YM Square Harajuku comprises a glass skin and vertical mullions, placing stores in full view of passersby and motorists.

Passageways (above) encourage use of the center as a shortcut to neighboring streets. Clear glass (right) is in abundance, making the tight, multilevel, half-acre site more spacious.

Cutouts allow natural light to flow into lower floors.

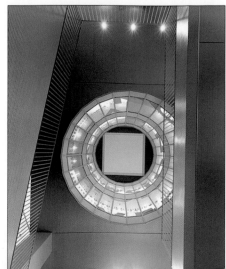

street, which features upscale retailers. The project also provides easy access to surrounding streets, attracting potential shoppers who seek a shortcut to their destination.

Stairs and escalators were located to increase traffic flow. Partly due to the project's location in a residential zone, the rear of the building had to be set back to meet Japanese sunshine regulations. This space was put to effective use by transforming it into open terraces where customers can relax in the open air.

Wooden deck floors in the open areas, including in the public places on the first floor and the terraces above, also extend into the stores to create a pleasant walking surface. A glass cylinder cuts through the upper floors to the open roof, allowing greater natural light into the center of the building.

One of the most challenging tasks in developing the site was the short construction schedule. The designer said that a project this size, with two basement floors and six above-ground floors, would typically have needed 20

Despite the tight site, stores (above left) are spacious. The gelato store (above) has seating outside. A street entrance (left) offers an escalator to whisk shoppers to retailers.

Generous use of glass and clear sight lines maximize the impact of retail displays.

months. In order to avoid the impact of new legislation (which would have had a detrimental impact on the project's development), the center had to open by January 31, 2001. Using a construction process that allowed simultaneous construction above ground and below, the project was built in 10½ months.

A theme of a "global flagship community" attracted international retailers. A French cosmetics company opened its first directly operated salon, which is also its largest store outside of France. A Japanese chain of over 40 furniture/homeware stores established its largest store in the nation. One of Japan's largest lingerie manufacturers opened a store. There are two Italian eateries, one specializing in health food and the other in gelatos, with over 100 flavors available.

Since the project's opening, there has been widespread interest from car companies, broadcasters and others for using the first floor's open space for promotional events. With its prime location, busy traffic and spots for gathering and relaxation, YM Square Harajuku says it is exceeding its own expectations.

MAJOR TENANTS

NAME	TYPE	GLA (SQ. FT.)
Sephora	Cosmetics	16,017
Fran Franc	Home furnishing	14,107
Venire Venire	Italian restaurant	7,489
Subito	Inner-wear fashion	1,901
Donatello's	Cafe	517

Innovative Design and Construction of a New Project

A glass-enclosed space (at left, above) lets light stream in from the roof to lower retail floors.

YM Square Harajuku offers outside seating for respite from shopping.

Owner:
Old Mutual Life Assurance Company of South Africa
Cape Town, Western Cape, Republic of South Africa

Management Company:
Old Mutual Properties (Pty) Ltd.
Cape Town, Western Cape, Republic of South Africa

Architect:
Bild Architects
Pretoria, Gauteng, Republic of South Africa

Designer:
Development Design Group, Inc.
Baltimore, Maryland, United States

General Contractor:
Wilson Bailey Homes (WBH)
Johannesburg, Gauteng, Republic of South Africa

Menlyn Park Shopping Centre
Pretoria, Guateng, Republic of South Africa

Gross size of center:
1,271,562 sq. ft.

Amount of space added or renovated:
639,489 sq. ft.

Gross leasable area excluding anchors:
673,450 sq. ft.

Total acreage of site:
56.5 acres

Type of center:
Super-regional center

Physical description:
Enclosed four-level mall

Location of trading area:
Suburban

Population:
- Primary trading area
  380,000

- Secondary trading area
  340,000

- Annualized percentage of shoppers anticipated to be from outside trade area
  15%

Development schedule:
- Original opening date
  October 1983

- Current expansion date
  February 2001

Parking spaces:
- Present number
  5,544

- 2,044 parking spaces added in renovation

*R*enovation of Menlyn Park in Pretoria, South Africa, doubled the size of the center, expanding it both horizontally and vertically, to create a shopping and entertainment venue.

Redesign and remerchandising sought to attract a wider customer market and to make vertical and horizontal movement within the project become seamless. To distinguish itself from other regional shopping centers in South Africa, highly thematic design has been combined with a palette of bright traditional South African colors and striking patterns. New lighting techniques, sculptural graphics and carefully planned tenant design criteria all add to the effectiveness of design.

The massive Menlyn Park renovation and expansion in South Africa dominates the scene from air or ground.

Signage clearly marks entrance and anchor locations.

Sporting events (above) and unobstructed views (right) add to the festival atmosphere.

MAJOR TENANTS		
NAME	TYPE	GLA (SQ. FT.)
Hyperama	Department store	215,485
Woolworths	Supermarket	70,752
Edgars	Department store	69,202
Nu Metro Theatres	Cinemas	68,125

Menlyn Park features four halls. Celestial Hall (left) shows the southern constellations. The Grand Hall (below) looks toward the outdoor events deck.

Working from a new master plan, existing partial upper levels were finally completed. A new upper floor was added and what had been a service tunnel became a new lower floor. A new ring road enhances traffic circulation and provides entry into a six-level parking garage. Entry points are now better identified and the new garage feeds directly into each of the center's four levels. The design transformed the top level of the garage into the Menlyn Drive-In, South Africa's first drive-in movie theater (located next to a new 16-screen cineplex).

Aviary Hall before (above) and after (facing page) shows the impact of imaginative design

Contributing entertainment to the shopping experience are four themed halls. Aviary Hall holds a two-story cage for 300 exotic birds. Celestial Hall uses fiber-optic lighting to display the southern constellations on the ceiling. Cavendish Hall offers the latest in fashion trends. The three-level Grand Hall has a tensile roof that adds to its open and airy ambience and a suspended catwalk-like structure that can carry the load of a car or aircraft. More entertainment can be found at Menlyn Events, a multipurpose arena inspired by Roman amphitheaters, which provides a venue for concerts, family-oriented attractions and sports events. Development Design Group, Inc., has a U.S. patent pending on the Events Deck and Drive-In above a parking garage.

Since much of the new space was achieved through expansion, existing stores felt minimal impact during construction. Carving through three levels to build the Grand Hall did require relocation of some tenants, who were moved to a designated "hospital zone" to continue trade during the renovation.

Informative signage in and around the center kept customers and tenants aware of construction progress. The public read about it through advertising in newspapers and other media. The ads prompted press coverage of all major steps of the renovation.

The garage's roof (top) became South Africa's first drive-in theater, with the screen visible to passersby (facing page). A circus (right) performs at the Menlyn Events arena.

Hopscotch, a moment's rest and snacking all await the shopper at Menlyn Park.

Professional safety personnel were on-hand 24 hours a day, and demolition work was always done after hours to minimize impact on shoppers. Construction areas were corded off and new walkways clearly marked. The architect's scale model was on display and shoppers got information from a full-time on-site information group: the "A-team."

The developer takes pride in the fact that the new Menlyn Park Shopping Centre has attracted other developers from Europe and the U.S. who come to view this combination of shopping and entertainment.

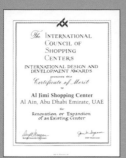

Al Jimi
Shopping Center

Al Ain, Abu Dhabi Emirate
United Arab Emirates

Owner:
Al Ain Municipal Authority
Al Ain, Abu Dhabi Emirate
United Arab Emirates

Management Company and Developer:
Addar Real Estate Services LLC
Abu Dhabi, Abu Dhabi Emirate
United Arab Emirates

Architect/Designer:
KEO International Consultants
Kuwait City, Kuwait

General Contractor:
Pivot Engineering and General Contracting Co.
Abu Dhabi, Abu Dhabi Emirate
United Arab Emirates

Gross size of center:
495,000 sq. ft.

Amount of space added or renovated:
190,000 sq. ft.

Gross leasable area excluding anchors:
340,000 sq. ft.

Total acreage of site:
5 acres

Type of center:
Regional center

Physical description:
Two-level

Location of trading area:
Suburban

Population:
- Primary trading area
  350,000

- Secondary trading area
  50,000

- Annualized percentage of shoppers
  anticipated to be from outside trade area
  5 – 10%

Development schedule:
- Original opening date
  September 1986

- Current expansion date
  May 2001

- Future expansion
  April 2003

Parking spaces:
- Present number
  1,500

- 730 parking spaces added in renovation

Al Jimi Shopping Center is the first regional shopping center in Al Ain, a few hours' drive from Abu Dhabi and Dubai. Completed in 1986, the original project ("Markaz Al Jimi") was a multilevel fruit, vegetable and meat market, the first commercial venture outside the traditional town-center commercial trading area. Limited parking and long pedestrian and vehicular ramps caused the market to cease operations within a year. The building fell into disrepair and remained dormant for many years.

The exciting exterior of Al Jimi Shopping Center (top) attracts residents for shopping and entertainment. The old center (left) had been unused for years and had fallen into disrepair. The new center (below) evolved with Carrefour's commitment to anchor.

*Old views (left)
and new (right)
illustrate
beautiful design
improvements.*

The developer secured the commitment of Carrefour, a large hypermarket, to anchor a new center on the site. The new anchor, renovation of the entire building, a 35-percent expansion in space, feature entrances and outdoor restaurant areas attracted a variety of tenants.

The opening of Al Jimi changed shoppers' habits by letting them shop near home. Previously, residents of Al Ain had to rely on the limited shops in their downtown or spend weekends shopping several hours away in Dubai and Abu Dhabi. The first floor of the center now houses brand-name fashion tenants, fast-food operators and two restaurants. Other tenants specialize in Arabic clothing, cosmetics and specialty items. There is a children's entertainment area — the first in the area.

An architectural rendering (above) shows the high priority given to parking and easy access. Renderings (below, left and right) indicate the subtlety of signage within the center.

A dazzling ceiling and beautiful tile floors provide accents to the design of Al Jimi Shopping Center, as revealed in these architectural renderings.

As the climate permits outdoor dining from late autumn through early spring, the restaurants were located to provide outdoor seating areas offering panoramic views of the palm groves and Jebel Hafeet mountains. Local architecture and design were accommodated in deciding internal and external finishes and the refurbishment of two feature water towers to resemble incense burners. The center maintains the strict guidelines of Islamic integrity in design and operation.

Water features and native palm trees are part of exterior design.

External signage and entryways are deliberately simple in design.

The access and egress roads to the center were significantly improved. The number of parking spaces increased from 730 to 1,500. For two months prior to opening, the center conducted a campaign to establish its logo and brand name, using media advertising, outdoor signs and branded directional signs throughout the city. A new Web site provided additional information. Subsequent marketing campaigns have ranged from "scratch-and-win" promotions to all-expense-paid overseas trips.

Work on the second phase of the center is marked for conclusion in April 2004. "Travelators" between floors, to facilitate trolley movement, will be added in the expansion. The next phase will also add more entertainment and leisure activity to the center, enhancing Al Jimi's role as a community center for the city of Al Ain.

The food court provides eating options. A storefront (below) communicates in two languages.

MAJOR TENANTS		
NAME	**TYPE**	**GLA (SQ. FT.)**
Carrefour	Hypermarket	75,000
Foton Edutainment	Entertainment	53,000
JC Penney	Department store	10,000
Shoe City	Mass merchandiser	9,000

Certificate of Merit

Owner:
ONTREA Inc.
Toronto, Ontario, Canada

Management Company:
Cadillac Fairview Corporation
Toronto, Ontario, Canada

Architect:
Petroff Partners Architects
Toronto, Ontario, Canada

Designer:
Pappas Design Studio
Montreal, Québec, Canada

General Contractor:
Vanbots
Toronto, Ontario, Canada

Hillcrest Mall

Richmond Hill, Ontario, Canada

Gross size of center:
577,134 sq. ft.

Amount of space added or renovated:
24,000 sq. ft.

Gross leasable area excluding anchors:
244,122 sq. ft.

Total acreage of site:
45.82 acres

Type of center:
Community center

Physical description:
One-level enclosed mall

Location of trading area:
Suburban

Population:
- Primary trading area
  180,056
- econdary trading area
  221,280
- Annualized percentage of shoppers anticipated to be from outside trade area
  11%

Development schedule:
- Original opening date
  January 1974
- Current expansion date
  December 2000

Parking spaces:
- Present number
  3,255

*H*illcrest Mall was opened in 1974 and had a minor renovation in 1990. Increasing competition, an aging look and inability to attract strong national retailers, particularly fashion retailers, called for its renovation and expansion. The goals were to enhance the mall's look and upgrade its retail merchandise mix.

Extensive market research prior to design work included focus groups, trade-area studies, license plate surveys and demographic and psychographic analyses. The results documented the need for widespread renovation and re-leasing.

Photos (above and opposite): Yves Lefebvre

A bold entryway (above) replaced an outdated entrance (left) at Hillcrest Mall.

A dull white ceiling (right) made way for elegant arches and enhanced lighting (facing page).

New streetscapes and inviting entrances now lead to a warm and timeless shopping environment. National retailers signed on, including GAP, Guess, Mexx, Nine West, Jacob and many others. In all, the center added 23 new stores and renovated 27 others, including eight that were expanded.

Construction entailed the removal of the existing common-area ceiling, including asbestos removal. A new ceiling, new lighting and new flooring were added. Exterior work included new portico entrances, new landscaping and reworking of the parking lot to improve traffic flow.

The mall was in full operation throughout the 10-month renovation. To ensure safety, signs at all main entrances let customers know about the current construction phase. Scaffolding supports were padded and side supports tarped to prevent young children from climbing. Temporary tenant signs were placed under the scaffolding to aid customers in finding stores. Podiums at key locations updated customers on construction details and store relocation. Hoarding directed traffic where sight lines were blocked. Overhead signs steered customers to key areas such as the food court, which was being relocated.

Brighter lighting (above) illuminates strong storefront design and offers an improvement on the former design (below).

Wood, lights and soft earth tones (left and facing page) give character to design.

Photos (above, left and opposite): Yves Lefebvre

Photo: *Yves Lefebvre*

The new design and leasing concepts attracted national retailers to the mall.

Further enhancements included the addition of 13 carpeted soft seating areas, with leather couches and chairs, tables, lamps and plants — rather than the wooden benches that were being replaced. An undecorated whitewash ceiling made way for an overhead design that complements the overall look. A rest room designed for the special needs of families offers both a separate nursing area and an enclosed children's playroom. A new customer-service kiosk serves as a prototype for those soon to be placed at other malls. Light earth tones now dominate the color palette. Suspended fixtures replaced recessed lighting.

Food court design complements the overall look.

MAJOR TENANTS		
NAME	**TYPE**	**GLA (SQ. FT.)**
Zellers	Department store	117,308
Bay Fashion Store	Department store	98,450
Bay Home & Kids	Department store	72,950
Good Life Fitness	Sports/fitness	22,792
Sport Chek	Sports/fitness	19,270

Soft seating, tables and lamps offer a homelike oasis during a shopping visit to Hillcrest Mall.

The renovation of Hillcrest Mall has led to the success of new and old retailers by attracting new shoppers from the quickly growing market.

Certificate of Merit

Owner and Management Company:

Simon Property Group, Inc.
Indianapolis, Indiana, United States

Architect/Designer:

RTKL Associates Inc.
Dallas, Texas, United States

General Contractor:

DPMI
Youngstown, Ohio, United States

NorthEast Mall

Hurst, Texas, United States

Gross size of center:
1,672,000 sq. ft.

Gross leasable area excluding anchors:
361,161 sq. ft.

Total acreage of site:
83.3 acres

Type of center:
Regional center

Physical description:
Enclosed mall

Location of trading area:
Suburban

Population:
- Primary trading area
  219,905

- Secondary trading area
  201,459

- Annualized percentage of shoppers
  anticipated to be from outside trade area
  0%

Development schedule:
- Original opening date
  March 11, 1971

- Current expansion date
  September 1, 2000

Parking spaces:
- Present number
  7,369

- 1,835 parking spaces added in
  renovation

A new look for a well-established center: NorthEast Mall in Hurst, Texas.

Built in the 1970s, NorthEast Mall in Hurst, Texas, northeast of Fort Worth, had been marketed to middle- and lower-income clientele. In the years since, the surrounding area had trended toward greater affluence and sophistication, triggering extensive renovation and expansion. Unlike its sister city of Dallas, the developer said, Fort Worth had no regional malls that were truly upscale in design or tenant mix. The developer sought to expand the mall's market draw, continue to serve the current customers and give the mall environment a conceptual hook.

Each of the mall's three wings has a unique design identity: either water, breeze or arbor.

New parking decks
contain concrete
bas-relief spandrel
panels, tying in to
the garden concept.

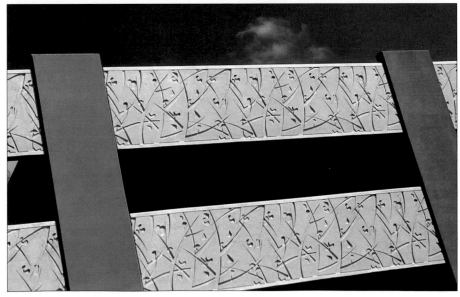

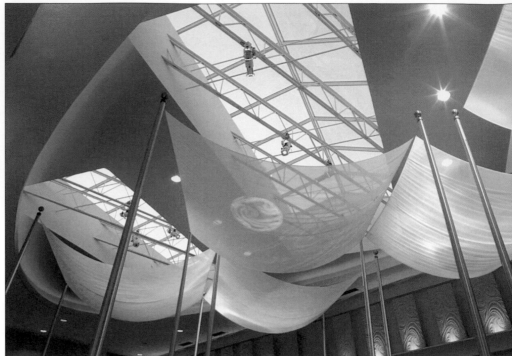

Dated lighting, colors and bulkhead forms (left column) called for a new approach.

Billowing translucent fabric and theatrical lighting decorate the ceiling of the Breeze Court.

MAJOR TENANTS

NAME	TYPE	GLA (SQ. FT.)
Dillards	Department store	350,022
JC Penney	Department store	237,887
Foley's	Department store	216,000
Sears	Department store	169,241
Nordstrom	Department store	142,439
Saks Fifth Avenue	Department store	100,352

Design excitement enhances both the new upscale retailers and the mix of retained tenants.

The renovation was driven by the desire of anchors like Nordstrom and Saks Fifth Avenue to locate in fast-growing Tarrant County. The redesign had to suit their customers and reflect their level of quality to attract similar types of anchors. Initial studies suggested an upper-level expansion, but it proved too costly to undertake. Instead, the developer opted to expand on grade by acquiring adjacent property.

To transform the image of the mall, the design and development team created a new "story line" upon which design decisions would be based: a notably "un-gardenlike" center at the intersection of highways would be transformed into an eclectic "garden party." By working abstractly with this literal concept, the designers blended trees, grass, flowers, light and even breeze to create a variety of themes that ranged from the gardens at Versailles to the backyard picnic.

A well-designed information booth attracts more customers.

The mall expanded to include a third wing, and each wing took a design concept of either breeze, water or arbor. A new mall concourse ceiling incorporated existing skylights. Bathed in blue light, the new ceiling gently curves to create a "perpetual sky." New limestone flooring shows a random size and color pattern, invoking a garden path. Bas-relief panels on the upper walls of each court have patterns and colors that reinforce the theme of breeze, water or arbor in that court.

Floor tiles in the food court were made from photographs of grass; the paving pattern was similar to what a lawnmower would create. In the common areas, hundreds of terracotta pots with plants evoke a Mediterranean-village pattern. In the Saks court, fountains are animated by backyard sprinklers gently swaying back and forth over the grass "lawns." Even the new parking decks tie into the garden design, with whimsical graphic patterns of trees and deep-green deck columns.

The center court (above) has an open look, with plenty of natural light. The randomness of color and size in the floor tiles (below) suggests a garden path.

The food court at NorthEast Mall benefits from bold graphics and a grand scale.

The team considered a new name for the mall, but stuck with the existing name because of its strong resonance in the community. A new logo and typeface, along with extensive community outreach, communicated change.

In addition to the new department stores, new tenants include J. Crew, Abercrombie and Fitch, Guess, Godiva, Banana Republic and others, thus meeting NorthEast Mall's goal of serving new upscale customers while also satisfying existing shoppers.

Photos ©Whitcomb/RTKL

Certificate of Merit

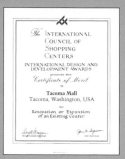

Owner and Management Company:
Simon Property Group, Inc.
Indianapolis, Indiana, United States

Architect:
EJD & Associates Co.
Youngstown, Ohio, United States

Designer:
Callison
Seattle, Washington, United States

General Contractor:
DPMI
Youngstown, Ohio, United States

Tacoma Mall

Tacoma, Washington, United States

Gross size of center:
1,248,576 sq. ft.

Amount of space added or renovated:
114,336 sq. ft.

Gross leasable area excluding anchors:
319,111 sq. ft.

Total acreage of site:
90 acres

Type of center:
Super-regional center

Physical description:
Enclosed one-level mall

Location of trading area:
Urban but not downtown

Population:
- Primary trading area
  428,707

- Secondary trading area
  N/A

- Annualized percentage of shoppers
  anticipated to be from outside trade area
  23%

Development schedule:
- Original opening date
  October 1965

- Current expansion date
  April 2000

Parking spaces:
- Present number
  6,732

Photo ©David Hewitt/Anne Garrison

*N*ewly renovated shopping malls and many new "big-box" retailers had been eroding Tacoma Mall's productivity in recent years. The tenant mix did not provide enough selection to support the upscale market. The mall's department stores were seeing expenditures that were higher than the national average, which indicated a general dissatisfaction with the in-line tenants. Finally, an old look, featuring dated Fritz tile, routine built-in planter/bench combinations and yellowed skylights, further indicated it was time for a change.

The new mall entrances (above and far right) stylishly and boldly announce the names of the center and its anchors, replacing the anonymous old entrance (near right).

A pylon at
Tacoma Mall is
updated.

Photos (below and far right)
©David Hewitt/Anne Garrison

A lackluster mall entrance (above) is turned into a beacon (right) for the new food court (facing page). Columns (bottom) were dressed up with sconces as design accents.

The Tacoma Mall renovation involved extensive refurbishment of the mall and the addition of a food court to the 33-year-old center. While the renovation budget would not accommodate major structural changes, an inviting park-like setting was created through design.

The most significant cosmetic changes included stone and stone-like flooring and new seating areas enhanced by overhead trellises, decorative sconces and

Photos (above, below and opposite) ©David Hewitt/Anne Garrison

Photos (above and opposite) © David Hewitt/Anne Garrison

An unchanged storefront (above left) can be enhanced by placing a sitting area in front.

light fixtures. A new paint scheme was used and new clear skylight lenses replaced the old yellow ones.

The mall had not previously had a food court, so one was carved out of space that originally housed a grocery/drugstore but was now 80 percent vacant except for temporary leases. At first, the developer was concerned about the location of the food court, nearly 200 feet off the main mall concourse. Once the commitment was made to that area, designers used bold signage, special lighting and floor tile patterns in the main walkway to draw people to the food court.

Once there, shoppers saw the food court's cool, calm water-tone colors and a welcoming space to relax and eat. The youngest shoppers enjoy a soft play area surrounded by a colorful handpainted mural with nautical

Ceilings, floors, wall murals, chairs — all can communicate thoughtful design.

MAJOR TENANTS		
NAME	**TYPE**	**GLA (SQ. FT.)**
Bon Marche	Department store	260,582
JC Penney	Department store	231,780
Sears	Department store	179,320
Nordstrom	Department store	131,633
Mervyn's	Department store	126,150

themes. The new food court reenergized a 60,000 square foot area of the mall — the area in and around the food court is now 100-percent leased. This aspect proved to the developers that a food court can pull people through a mall and act as an anchor.

Major seismic reinforcement — sizable in-fill arches between rows of columns — burdened the mall's center court. Costs prohibited replacement of the arches and columns, so they were turned into a design element by dressing them up with a stone-like finish and sconces.

The interior mall renovation was done at nighttime, after the stores had closed. The mall used barricades and information signage to help protect shoppers in the construction areas. There was actually a 10-percent increase in foot traffic in the mall during the renovation process.

The renovation attracted national retailers from the most-desired categories: children's apparel, women's upscale apparel, sporting goods and food. Old Navy, Victoria's Secret, Abercrombie Kids, Ann Taylor Loft, Finish Line and the nine food court tenants placed Tacoma Mall squarely in the market it sought through renovation.

A soft play area with nautical themes entertains the youngest shoppers at Tacoma Mall.

Certificate of Merit

Owner and Management Company:

Simon Property Group, Inc.
Indianapolis, Indiana, United States

Architect:

DPMI
Youngstown, Ohio, United States

Designer:

RTKL Associates Inc.
Dallas, Texas, United States

General Contractors:

DPMI
Youngstown, Ohio, United States

Town Center at Boca Raton

Boca Raton, Florida, United States

Gross size of center:
1,559,606 sq. ft.

Gross leasable area excluding anchors:
492,309 sq. ft.

Total acreage of site:
123 acres

Type of center:
Super-regional center

Physical description:
Enclosed mall

Location of trading area:
Urban but not downtown

Population:
- Primary trading area
  466,270

- Secondary trading area
  534,009

- Annualized percentage of shoppers
  anticipated to be from outside trade area
  25%

Development schedule:
- Original opening date
  August 1980

- Current expansion date
  November 3, 2000

Parking spaces:
- Present number
  7,874

- 902 parking spaces added in renovation

*T*own Center at Boca Raton is a super-regional shopping center serving two affluent Florida counties. Last renovated over a decade earlier, the center had begun to feel dated: low light levels, outmoded tenant criteria and dark and uneven tile floors. The food court was too small for the growing number of customers and navigating the long mall was not easy. The center could support more high-end retailers, so the plan was to attract them through renovation.

Two existing anchors were expanded and one added. Renovation included entrances, all finishes, lighting and new parking structures. The mall store area was expanded by a half-million square feet, accommodating 60 new shops and an enlarged food court.

Palm trees (above) are a logical design component for Town Center at Bacon Raton. Mall entrances that had been hidden before (right) are clearly identified now (below).

Greenery abounds in the new design, as does new seating and natural light.

Water features and plantings bring the verdant Florida environment inside the mall.

MAJOR TENANTS

NAME	TYPE	GLA (SQ. FT.)
Saks Fifth Avenue	Department store	332,676
Bloomingdale's	Department store	264,300
Burdines	Department store	216,000
Nordstrom	Department store	170,200
Sears	Department store	167,600
Lord & Taylor	Department store	110,400

Fortunately, the original design and subsequent changes used simple volumes of space. Large pyramidal skylights, circular courts and a pitched linear skylight gallery all contributed to a palette that could be repainted and enhanced without drastic changes to structure. The principal challenge was in what to keep and what to replace.

The renovation and expansion introduced a lighter, airier design to the center. A palm tree motif and new water features reflected the regional environment. A light-colored stone floor with carpet inserts was installed. Drywall ceilings in light hues with colored accents helped update the mall area. Elegant light fixtures were added. Entrances were totally rebuilt to feature architectural towers flanked by glass storefronts to better connect the interior and exterior.

The food court was expanded and enlivened with bolder graphics.

The reconfigured food court allowed more seating and better circulation. The visibility and character of food court tenants was enhanced by environmental graphics, including fabrics printed with vintage floral patterns that related to the center's design concept.

Because the renovation was done after hours, it neither interfered with regular business nor endangered shoppers. Construction areas were closed off with white picket fences, rather than yellow tape. Tenants were relocated, so no shops were closed. The center was draped, inside and out, with message boards and banners advertising new stores.

Way-finding signage helps shoppers on their way through the mall.

Comfortable seating encourages longer shopping visits than had the empty mall walkway in the old design (below).

Food traffic increased during the renovation, as customers brought friends to see what would happen to "their" mall. A sale of plants, benches and Mexican floor tiles from the previous design let consumers take a little piece of Town Center history home with them.

Finally, an updated graphics package brought directional clarity to shoppers' visits. The center is essentially a big circle, and way-finding graphics help shoppers orient themselves from the moment they enter the parking lot. In all, design, graphics and new retailers brought Town Center at Boca Raton up to date with its upscale market.

Graphics are clear but discreet at the new Town Center at Boca Raton.

Photos ©Whitcomb/RTKL